Introduction

Cathedrals serve a wide community. A cathedral houses the throne, the seat – or, in Latin, *cathedra* – of the bishop, making it a centre for Christian worship and teaching, and the Christian mission. Cathedrals also act as important meeting places for people and ideas; they are centres for the arts, learning and public debate. Situated in the nation's capital, St Paul's is London's cathedral and embodies the spiritual life and heritage of the British people.

The present St Paul's is the fifth cathedral to have stood on the site since 604, and was built between 1675 and 1711, after its predecessor was destroyed in a fire. This was the first cathedral to be built after the English Reformation in the sixteenth century, when Henry VIII removed the Church of England from the jurisdiction of the Pope and the Crown took control of the Church's life.

Today the Church of England describes herself as catholic and reformed. She has bishops and priests, and celebrates Baptism and the Eucharist in the traditional manner. But her worship has always been in English, her priests are permitted to marry, and both women and men are ordained. Cathedrals are perhaps the ultimate expression of the inclusiveness of the Church of England, seeking to serve all people, irrespective of their status or faith.

OPPOSITE: **view towards the altar and the quire beyond**
BELOW: **worship under the dome**

History

From being one of the first fledgling Christian settlements to becoming an icon of the Christian faith in Britain, St Paul's has changed and grown to reflect the tastes, attitudes and people of the nation. Buildings have been constructed and have fallen, services have changed and been updated, but throughout its history St Paul's has remained a busy working church.

604: The first St Paul's

St Paul's overlooks the City of London, the heart of the capital. The City covers just one square mile and is almost a state within a state, clinging proudly to its status and traditions.

There have been churches and religious monuments on the site of St Paul's since Roman times. Sir Christopher Wren recorded that, when excavations for his building began, 'We discovered Quantities of Urns, bro-

ken Vessels and Pottery-ware… [the site] manifestl shew'd a great Antiquity.'

In 604 the first cathedral dedicated to St Paul wa built on the site by Mellitus, Bishop of the East Saxons This first wooden building burned down in 675 and wa rebuilt ten years later, only to be destroyed by the Viking in 962. A new church was then built in stone.

1087: Old St Paul's

Following a fire in 1087, the church was rebuilt again. The Normans who had recently conquered Britain were determined to create the longest and tallest Christian church in the world. It was finished in 1240, but enlarge ment work began less than twenty years later and the cathedral was finally consecrated in 1300.

Over the centuries the Norman cathedral fell into dis repair. After investigations were commissioned in the early

seventeenth century, restoration finally began in 1633, under Inigo Jones. The nave and transepts were refaced in Portland stone in a classical style, and the west front was remodelled with a portico. In 1642, however, the English Civil War put a stop to further work on what was arguably the most important classical building in the country.

During the Civil War and the subsequent Republic, which followed the execution of King Charles I in 1649, the country became less respectful towards the established Church. Many places of worship were allowed to become dilapidated, including St Paul's, which was used for stabling horses and the nave became a market-place, with a road running through the transepts.

When the monarchy was restored in 1660, King Charles II threw out the traders and began to return the scarred cathedral to its former status. In 1662 the quire was fitted out for services while the rest of the building was repaired. A year later a royal commission was established to examine the state of the building, and Christopher Wren was asked to prepare plans for restoration.

Wren's plan was accepted in August 1666, but before he had a chance to start work the Great Fire of London intervened.

1666: The Great Fire of London

The blaze started on 2 September and destroyed two-thirds of the City of London. It burned for four days and nights, destroying 13,200 houses and 87 parish churches, as well as old St Paul's. Miraculously, fewer than 20 people lost their lives.

King Charles and the Lord Mayor quickly appointed a new commission to organise the reconstruction of the City, and just nine days after the start of the fire Wren produced a plan. It was a celebration of light, with streets radiating out from key buildings and squares like rays of sunshine. The plan also incorporated a design for a new cathedral, with golden stone and clear glass windows and gold paintwork.

Unfortunately for Wren, the City's occupants – who needed places to live and work as soon as possible – began their own rebuilding work almost at once, and his plan for the City never came to fruition.

Temporary repairs were also made to old St Paul's, but the structure was fundamentally unsound. Finally, in 1668, Wren was asked to produce a design for a new building. Demolition of the old cathedral began the same year.

Sir Christopher Wren

Wren was an extraordinary figure. Although he is now best known as an architect, he was also an astronomer, scientist and mathematician.

Wren was a founder member in 1660 of the Royal Society, a national academy for science, but he was also a man of profound Christian faith. He came from a family of clergy who had been loyal to the Royalist cause during the Civil War, and it was faith that inspired his thought. 'Architecture', he once explained, 'aims at eternity.'

As an architect favoured by royalty and state, Wren's commissions varied widely. They included the Greenwich Observatory and Greenwich Hospital, and extensive work at Hampton Court Palace and Kensington Palace, as well as some magnificent buildings in Oxford, where he studied and worked as Professor of Astronomy from 1661 to 1673.

However, Wren's great passion was for the City of London, for St Paul's and for the many City churches he designed following the Great Fire.

1669–75: The designs

Wren produced his first design for St Paul's in 1669. This was rejected, however, on the grounds that it was too 'foreign' and insufficiently traditional. Then, in 1673, Charles II commissioned rebuilding work, using a second design by Wren as a guide. This plan was based on the shape of a Greek cross – with four arms of equal length. The King also commissioned the Great Model (now housed in the cathedral's Trophy Room), based on a third design, evolved from the Greek cross and intended to provide an 'unchangeable rule and direction' for the work.

This design was also abandoned, however, because the authorities did not have enough money to pay for all the work at once and it could not be built in stages. The Dean and Chapter – the clergy of St Paul's – also insisted that the cathedral should follow the conventional pattern of a Latin cross, with one section, the nave, longer than the rest.

A final design, known as the Warrant Design, was given royal approval on 14 May 1675 and featured a dome to satisfy the architect, but topped with a tall spire and set on a Latin cross to satisfy the Dean and Chapter. Wren's son wrote: 'The Surveyor resolved to make no more Models, or publickly expose his Drawings, which (as he had found by Experience) did but lose Time, and subjected his Business many Times to incompetent Judges.'

In the 1675 warrant the King gave Wren the freedom to 'make some variations, rather ornamental, than essential, as from Time to Time he should see proper'. Wren took full advantage, changing the proportions of the building and abandoning the idea of a spire on top of the dome. Today's cathedral, therefore, is very different from the agreed design.

1675–1711: The birth of the new St Paul's

The first building contracts were confirmed in July 1675. Just thirty-six years later building work was finished, making St Paul's the first English cathedral to be completed during the lifetime of the original architect.

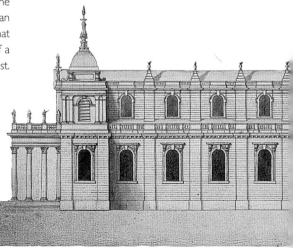

/3

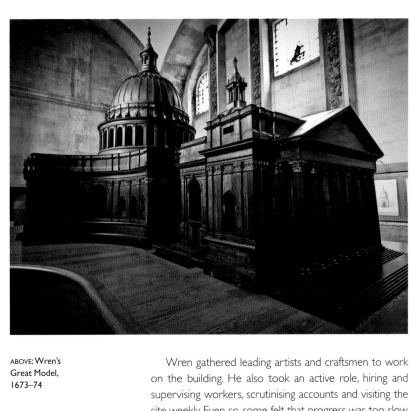

ABOVE: Wren's
Great Model,
1673–74

Wren gathered leading artists and craftsmen to work on the building. He also took an active role, hiring and supervising workers, scrutinising accounts and visiting the site weekly. Even so, some felt that progress was too slow. In 1697 the commissioning committee put pressure on Wren by persuading Parliament to withhold half his salary until the building was finished.

The quire opened for worship on 2 December 1697, while building work continued around it. The cathedral was completed in 1711. Until his death, at the age of ninety-one, Wren regularly returned to St Paul's to sit under the dome and reflect on this masterpiece of faith and imagination.

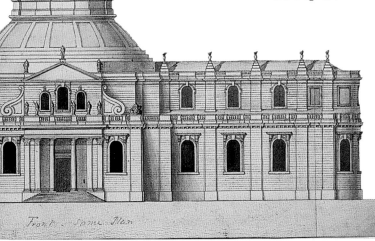

LEFT: Wren's
Warrant Design,
1675

A tradition of public service

In the same year as the quire opened, St Paul's held its first event of national importance – a thanksgiving service following war between England and France. For over 300 years since then St Paul's has been a place where the individual and the nation can express those feelings of joy, gratitude and sorrow that are so central to our lives.

Among the events marked at St Paul's are royal occasions. As our head of state, the King or Queen, and their family, are wrapped up in the events of the nation and their personal celebrations are often remembered publicly at St Paul's.

In the late eighteenth century a service was held to celebrate the return to good health of George III following a period of mental illness. In 1897 Queen Victoria chose to commemorate her diamond jubilee here, celebrating her sixtieth year on the throne. A sermon was preached on the cathedral steps while the 78-year-old queen sat nearby in her open carriage. More recently Queen Elizabeth II has celebrated her jubilees at St Paul's and also her 80th birthday in 2006. Royal weddings have been held here as well: the marriage of Catherine of Aragon to Prince Arthur in 1501 and famously the wedding of HRH the Prince of Wales to Lady Diana Spencer in 1981.

As the nation's church, St Paul's has also been the site of state funerals of British military leaders, including Admiral Lord Nelson and the Duke of Wellington, and of the wartime Prime Minister, Sir Winston Churchill. Services have also been held to mark the valuable contributions made by ordinary men and women involved in armed conflicts in the Falklands, the Gulf and Northern Ireland. A vast crowd also gathered at St Paul's following the terrorist attacks on New York on 11 September 2001, as London expressed its solidarity with the people of New York at a time of grief.

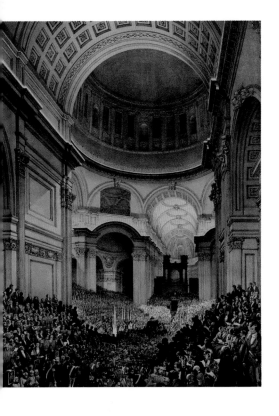

BELOW LEFT: thousands mourn at St Paul's following the September 11 bombings in New York
BELOW RIGHT: the wedding of Lady Diana Spencer and Prince Charles, 1981

OVERLEAF: Queen Victoria listens to an open-air service to celebrate her Diamond Jubilee

People of other faiths have a place in national services at St Paul's. The memorial service for King Hussein of Jordan in 1999 was the first Christian service in St Paul's to include a reading from the Qur'an. In 2005, at the service of remembrance following the terrorist bombings in London in July of that year, young people representing different faith communities lit candles as a shared sign of hope during turbulent times.

In these symbolic ways London's cathedral seeks to be a house of prayer for people of all nations. It is a place for protest against injustice and for the public expression of hope for a better society. Martin Luther King stopped to preach at St Paul's *en route* to collect his Nobel Peace Prize in 1964. Former Prime Minister, Gordon Brown, spoke at St Paul's when the G20 summit opened in London in 2009. Involvement in the global community and social justice are as much a part of the working life of St Paul's as prayer and ceremonial.

The Nave

The word 'nave' comes from the Latin word for a ship, an image often used to represent the Christian Church and to suggest the idea of a spiritual journey. The nave is where the members of the church gather. Here, and throughout the cathedral, memorials record the history of those who have gathered at St Paul's across the centuries.

The west end of the nave is dominated by the great West Doors, the ceremonial entrance reserved for the sovereign and for great occasions. The white marble font, carved by Francis Bird in 1726–27, is deliberately placed in front of these doors. The font is used for baptism, which marks the beginning of the journey of faith that Christians believe leads from earth to heaven.

On the north side of the nave is its most spectacular monument: to the Duke of Wellington, best known for the defeat of Napoleon at Waterloo in 1815. Wellington died in 1852 and is buried in the crypt.

At the head of the nave, just before it opens out into the dome area, stands the great lectern, part of the original

furnishings of the present building. The Word of God stands in our midst, held on the wings of the eagle, a bird of strength and vision.

OPPOSITE: gathering for worship in the nave
ABOVE: effigy of the Duke of Wellington
BELOW: memorial to General Charles Gordon

BELOW: memorial to Lord Kitchener
OPPOSITE: St Dunstan's Chapel, a place
for reflection

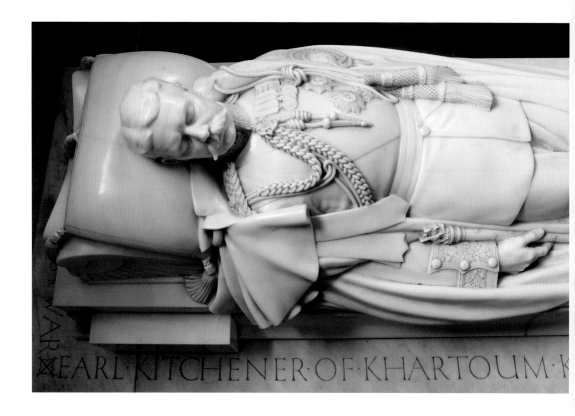

EARL·KITCHENER·OF·KHARTOUM·K

All Souls' Chapel: the Kitchener Memorial

This chapel was dedicated in 1925 to the memory of Field Marshal Lord Kitchener and the servicemen who died in the First World War. Kitchener died at sea, and his body was never recovered. He is best known for his restructuring of the British army during the First World War and for the most effective recruitment campaign in British military history, using the slogan 'Your Country Needs You!'

St Dunstan's Chapel

The chapel was consecrated in 1699, and is traditionally where the morning service of Mattins was conducted on weekdays, although other chapels are now also used for this purpose. In 1905 it was dedicated to St Dunstan, a Bishop of London who became the Archbishop of Canterbury in 959.

The silver pyx that hangs above the altar in this chapel contains the sacrament – the consecrated bread that Christians believe is the body of Jesus, shared at services of Holy Communion. The presence here of the sacrament gives this chapel particular importance; it is the place reserved for prayer and stillness. You can light a candle here, as a sign of prayer, and you can also leave the names of those you wish to be remembered in prayer during one of the cathedral's services.

The Chapel of St Michael and St George

This chapel was originally laid out as a consistory court in which cases of ecclesiastical law were heard. Renamed in 1906 and dedicated to St Michael and St George, it is the spiritual home of the Order of St Michael and St George, founded in 1818 to honour people who have rendered important service overseas.

Above the chapel stalls are banners of current knights and officers of the Order, including the Queen, who visits periodically for the Order's ceremonial service.

The Dome

St Paul's is built in the shape of a cross, with a large dome crowning the intersection of its arms – something unique among English cathedrals. At 111.3 metres high, it is one of the largest cathedral domes in the world and weighs approximately 65,000 tons. The area under the dome is the space where the most important work of the cathedral is done – its liturgy, or worship. The altar is the focus for this, as the place where the Eucharist is celebrated each Sunday. It becomes a symbol of unity for people of all ages and many different languages, who gather

OPPOSITE: looking up into the dome
BELOW: the dome topped with a ball and cross

to eat and drink the bread and wine that symbolise, by being offered to God in prayer, the body and blood of Jesus Christ.

St Paul's has a three-dome structure. This allows the inner dome to rise in proportion to the internal architecture, and the outer dome to be much larger and impressive. It is this outer dome shell that is prominent on the London skyline. The inner dome is the painted dome one sees looking up from the cathedral floor. Between these two domes is the third; a brick cone which provides strength and supports the stone lantern above.

Within the dome's construction there are three gallery levels. The whispering gallery runs around the interior of the dome. It is 157 steps up from ground level. The name derives from a charming acoustical quirk in the gallery's construction, which makes a whisper against its walls audible on the opposite side. Two higher galleries encircle the outside of the dome – the stone gallery and the smaller, golden gallery, which runs around the highest point of the outer dome at 528 steps from the cathedral floor. Both the stone and the golden galleries offer superb views across London.

ABOVE: mosaic of Isaiah, an Old Testament prophet
OPPOSITE: mural by James Thornhill, of St Paul shipwrecked in Malta

It has been suggested that Wren had intended to decorate the inside of the dome in mosaic. But in 1709 the cathedral commissioners appointed James Thornhill to paint it in monochrome, partly because mosaic was expensive, time-consuming and considered too elaborate.

Thornhill had made his name at Hampton Court Palace. He began work on the dome at St Paul's in 1715 and finished four years later. His murals are based on a series of pen-and-ink sketches on the life of St Paul. What we see today are reproductions from Thornhill's designs that were repainted in 1853. The originals deteriorated as a result of the British climate and London smog.

Further decoration of the dome area was added later. Filling the triangular spaces between the arches of the dome columns are mosaics depicting the Old Testament prophets Isaiah, Jeremiah, Ezekiel and Daniel, and the four evangelists, Matthew, Mark, Luke and John. These were designed by the artists Alfred Stevens and George Frederic Watts, and installed between 1864 and 1893.

The North Transept and Quire Aisle

At the end of the north transept is the Chapel of Saints Erkenwald and Ethelburga. This chapel is home to the Middlesex Regiment, whose flags are laid here.

Ethelburga was the Abbess of a powerful double monastery – for men and women. Her brother Erkenwald became Bishop of London in 675. He was much loved and believed to be a miracle worker. His tomb became a shrine in the former cathedral but was destroyed during the Reformation in the sixteenth century.

At the entrance to the north quire aisle is a statue of Samuel Johnson, placed there in 1796. It was paid for by a subscription started by the Literary Club, of which Dr Johnson was a founder member and which included many eminent writers, artists and actors of the time.

In the third bay of the north quire aisle is Henry Moore's *Mother and Child*. Moore himself chose the location for this work, a commission that he received in 1983, when he was recovering from an illness. It was one of the sculptor's last works, on a theme that is popular in his works and that takes on a religious meaning in this setting.

OPPOSITE: the dome crossing from the north transept
ABOVE: *Mother and Child* by Henry Moore
RIGHT: statue of Samuel Johnson by Johannes Bacon

Close to Moore's sculpture are two pairs of wrought-iron gates made by Jean Tijou around 1700, in the Baroque style.

William Holman Hunt's painting *The Light of the World* is now used as an altarpiece in the Chapel of Saints Erkenwald and Ethelburga. The painting dates from around 1900 and is the third version that Holman Hunt painted of the subject. This painting travelled the world in 1905 – it was considered an important painting with a strong spiritual message – to be seen by many and achieved celebrity status. It claims a place of recognition for Judaism and Islam in the light that shines from Jesus Christ. The Star of David and the Islamic crescent moon can be seen on the left side of the lamp that Jesus holds.

ABOVE: wrought-iron gates by Jean Tijou
RIGHT: detail of St Paul, the cathedral's patron
OPPOSITE: *Light of the World* by William Holman Hunt

THE
OF THE

LIGHT
WORLD

BEHOLD I STAND AT THE DOOR AND KNOCK IF ANY MAN
HEAR MY VOICE AND OPEN THE DOOR I WILL COME
IN TO HIM AND WILL SVP. WITH HIM AND HE WITH ME.

The Quire

The quire was the first part of the cathedral to be built and consecrated. It was originally separated from the rest of the cathedral by an elaborate screen with the organ fixed on top of it.

This original organ was made in 1694 by a renowned German organ builder, Bernard Schmidt. The composer George Frederick Handel loved playing this instrument, perhaps because, uniquely in Britain at the time, it had pedals. The organ has been rebuilt several times, most recently in 2008, when a second, movable, console was installed under the dome. The present organ is the third largest in the UK; it has 7,256 pipes, 5 manuals and 138 stops.

The organ case and stalls on both sides of the quire are decorated with exquisitely delicate carvings by the Anglo-Dutch sculptor Grinling Gibbons, whose work is seen in many royal palaces and great houses. One contemporary commentator wrote: *'There is no instance of a man before Gibbons who gave to wood the loose and airy lightness of flowers [...] with the free disorder natural to each species.'*

These stalls are still used daily for their original purpose. They are where the choir, clergy and people sit for Evensong, a service that gives thanks to God for the day as it draws to a close.

Each of the canopied stalls has a designated occupant. The Bishop of London's throne has the grandest canopy of all. The Lord Mayor of London also has a grand stall, while the other stalls reflect the pattern of how a cathedral is governed.

OPPOSITE: organ pipes on the north side of the quire
ABOVE: carved cherubim above the quire stalls

RIGHT: the Bishop's throne
OVERLEAF: view of the quire and the baldacchino beyond

The senior priest in the cathedral is the Dean. In addition, St Paul's has four priests and three laypeople who are canons and assist the Dean, forming the Chapter, which is the cathedral's governing body. Prebendaries serve at St Paul's; these are clergy who work in parishes and institutions in the diocese and whose task is to pray for the mission of St Paul's and the Church in London.

Queen Victoria once famously complained that St Paul's was 'dull, dingy and undevotional'. The mosaics that now decorate the ceiling and walls of the quire were installed in 1896–1904, in response to this remark, to a design by William Blake Richmond. The ceiling illustrates the song of creation, from the Old Testament, while the wall mosaics tell the story of the angel Gabriel visiting the Virgin Mary with the news that she will give birth to Jesus.

The present high altar and baldacchino, or canopy, dates from 1958, and are designed by John Dykes Bower to represent something of Wren's original intention. The previous Victorian altarpiece was destroyed in bomb damage during the Second World War.

OPPOSITE: mosaics above the quire, depicting Creation

ABOVE: the birds of the air mosaic
RIGHT: an angel mosaic

The Jesus Chapel:
The American Memorial Chapel

Behind the altar is the Jesus Chapel. As part of the post-war restoration it was decided that the people of Britain should commemorate the 28,000 Americans who were killed on their way to, or while stationed in, the UK during the Second World War. Their names are recorded in the 500-page roll of honour encased behind the high altar.

OPPOSITE: gilded statue of Jesus
on the top of the baldacchino
ABOVE: the American Memorial Chapel
INSET: the American roll of honour

The South Quire Aisle and Transept

In the south quire aisle is the effigy of John Donne, which miraculously survived the Great Fire of London intact. Donne, a former Dean of St Paul's, wrote passionate love poems, but in prose and poetry he also expressed with incomparable eloquence his passion for God. He is perhaps best remembered, though, for his meditation on the human condition, with its observation that 'No man is an island, entire of itself ... never send to ask for whom the bell tolls; it tolls for thee.'

The memorial to Admiral Lord Nelson is by the distinguished neo-classical sculptor John Flaxman, who began work on it three years after the subject's death. It was finished ten years later, in 1818. The monument shows a cloak covering the area where Nelson's right arm should be – the limb was amputated in 1797.

From the portico of the south transept there is a fine view over the Millennium Bridge towards Tate Modern and The Globe, a reconstructed Shakespearian theatre.

OPPOSITE: the south quire aisle or 'Dean's aisle'
ABOVE: shrouded effigy of John Donne
LEFT: statue of Admiral Lord Nelson

The Crypt

Three death-heads mark the entrance to the crypt, the burial chamber of the cathedral. The floor of the crypt was originally plain earth, in which coffins were simply buried with a stone placed on top. The Victorians began the tradition of viewing the crypt, and a proper floor was laid.

Lord Nelson was famously killed in the Battle of Trafalgar in 1805 and buried in St Paul's after a state funeral. He was laid in a coffin made from the timber of a French ship he defeated in battle. The black marble sarcophagus that adorns his tomb was originally made for Cardinal Wolsey, Lord Chancellor during the reign of Henry VIII in the early sixteenth century. After Wolsey's fall from favour, it remained unused at Windsor until a suitable recipient was found. Nelson's viscount coronet now tops this handsome monument.

Lord Wellington, the 'Iron Duke', rests in a simple but imposing casket of Cornish granite. Although a national hero, Wellington was not a man to glory in his victories. 'Nothing except a battle lost can be half so melancholy as a battle won', he wrote after Waterloo. Wellington's tomb is surrounded by the banners used in the funeral procession that brought him to St Paul's in 1852.

Like Wellington, Nelson valued not just the fact of victory in battle but also the manner of that victory and the quality of life that it afforded. Immediately prior to Trafalgar, Nelson's prayer was for 'humanity after victory'.

The crypt of St Paul's has monuments to conflicts and to other outstanding achievements in the cause of a better world. In some cases the names on these monuments are still cherished by loved ones. We are reminded of the human cost paid by those who have striven for what they believed in.

OPPOSITE: **tomb of Admiral Lord Nelson**
BELOW: **three death-heads above the entrance to the crypt**

The Chapel of St Faith, Chapel of the Order of the British Empire

The original St Faith's was a parish church attached to the old cathedral destroyed in the Great Fire of London. During the rebuilding of St Paul's, this chapel was dedicated to St Faith close to the foundations of the former church and offered the parishioners their own place of worship in the new building. In 1960 this chapel became the spiritual home to the Order of the British Empire.

The Order was created by King George V in 1917, in recognition especially of the contribution made by women during the First World War. Until then no woman had been eligible for an award, although an exception was made for Florence Nightingale, the founder of modern British nursing. The OBE was separated into military and civil divisions in 1918. Today, award-holders of the OBE and members of their family may be baptised and married in the chapel.

OPPOSITE: **tomb of the Duke of Wellington** BELOW: **the OBE Chapel**

Surrounding this chapel are memorials celebrating figures from the arts and sciences. These include the painters Joshua Reynolds, J. M. W. Turner and John Everett Millais, the composer Sir Arthur Sullivan and the poet William Blake. The scientist Sir Alexander Fleming, who discovered penicillin, is also commemorated in the north-west corner.

Sir Christopher Wren himself is buried in the south aisle of this chapel. His tomb is marked by a simple stone and is surrounded by memorials to his family, to Robert Hooke (Wren's associate and intellectual equal) and to the masons and other colleagues who worked on the building of St Paul's. The Latin epitaph above his tomb, written by his son famously addresses us: 'Reader, if you seek his monument, look around you.'

In the far right corner of the OBE Chapel is a monument to Randolph Caldecott (1846–1886). It shows a child holding a medallion with a bas-relief image of the Victorian book illustrator.

ABOVE: memorial to Florence Nightingale
RIGHT: memorial to Randolph Caldecott

The Exterior and Churchyard

The west front of St Paul's is dominated by a triangular relief depicting the conversion of the cathedral's patron saint to Christianity. Above it stands the figure of St Paul himself, flanked by other apostles and the four evangelists. This was the work of Francis Bird (in 1718–21), who was greatly influenced by the church architecture of Rome. Bird also carved the statue of Queen Anne that stands in front of St Paul's. Anne was the reigning monarch at the time of the cathedral's completion.

The two western towers are topped with a pineapple – a symbol of peace, prosperity and hospitality. Near the top of the south-west tower is a clock, which was installed in 1893 and has three faces, each more than 5 metres in diameter.

Above the clock hang Great Tom, the hour bell, and Great Paul, the largest swinging bell in Europe. Great Paul pre-dates the cathedral, while Great Tom was presented to the cathedral in 1716. Great Tom strikes the hours and tolls to mark the death of the Sovereign. The north-west tower houses the remaining twelve bells which sound the peal.

ABOVE: statue of Queen Anne in front of the cathedral, carved by Francis Bird
OPPOSITE: west front portico with relief carving of the evangelists by Francis Bird

OVERLEAF: view down Ludgate Hill with St Paul's towers, Great Tom (left) and Great Paul (right)

OPPOSITE: the south churchyard gardens, the site of the medieval chapter house

RIGHT: statue of St Paul in the north-east churchyard

BELOW: carved winged cherubs above the Dean's door in the south churchyard.

The south churchyard was refashioned in 2008. On the pavement at the western end of the churchyard is a floor-plan of the pre-Fire cathedral, with on outline of the present one superimposed on it. The older building was bigger!

Today the Chapter House, or administrative centre for the cathedral, stands on the north side: an elegant brick building that faces into the newly developed Paternoster Square, which used to be the centre of the printing trade.

Near by, in the cathedral's north-east churchyard, a plaque marks the location of Paul's Cross, a popular centre of news and comment, where during the Reformation William Tyndale's New Testament was burned because it was in English, and where generations of Londoners played their part in fomenting public opinion. The column mounted with a gilded statue of St Paul also commemorates the public preaching of the Christian faith in this location.

The Cathedral Today

St Paul's is a large complex organisation, employing around 200 staff and responsible for a similar number of volunteers, managing a significant portfolio of listed property, playing a key role in the tourist industry, taking a lead in music, conservation, design and education, and ready to respond at a moment's notice in the event of a major national or international event. Ultimately St Paul's is about people.

Worship and work

Vergers, stewards and a pastoral team of volunteer clergy from the Diocese of London minister throughout the week not only to pilgrims but also to tourists and visitors.

In addition to the daily round of worship, a team of three Minor Canons work with the Dean and Chapter to prepare and lead a wide range of services that

ABOVE: dancers perform under the dome
LEFT: choristers in the quire

celebrate special events in the life of the nation or ou national institutions, ranging from the Leonard Cheshir Foundation to Christian Aid and the US Thanksgivin Day Service.

Music

Music is a crucial element of daily worship and of life a St Paul's. Music transcends cultural barriers to become language of the human spirit that enables people of ever nation, whatever their background, to reach out to some thing beyond themselves.

The music at St Paul's, with its continuing tradition c innovation and inspiration, takes a leading role in Churc music worldwide. Dedicated to sustaining the vitalit of this tradition are the Director of Music, the organis sub-organist and organ scholar, eighteen adult singers known as the Vicars Choral — and about forty choristers

Education

Learning is a vital part of the cathedral's life and missior St Paul's Cathedral School was founded originally for th education of its choristers. It now has about 240 boys an girls, aged from four to thirteen, who are an integral par of the cathedral's life.

The cathedral's Education Department provides facili-es and programmes for the 25,000 schoolchildren who sit St Paul's each year.

The St Paul's Institute continues to engage Christianity vith the contemporary issues that challenge us globally nd personally. Speakers such as Kofi Annan, Sir David ttenborough and Bianca Jagger have discussed issues anging from the global economy to climate change.

ABOVE: a conservator cleans a model from the cathedral's collections
BELOW: a stone mason repairs weathered stone in the churchyard

Maintaining St Paul's

Repairing, restoring and embellishing the fabric of St Paul's are a labour of love, overseen by the Clerk of Works and his staff, under the expert guidance of the cathedral's Surveyor to the Fabric.

In addition to expert work on the fabric, a team skilled in conservation and collection management looks after the cathedral's historic collections – its library, archives, plate and textiles.

As part of St Paul's 300th anniversary campaign in 2008, £40 million were raised to repair and clean the cathedral both inside and out. State-of-the-art restoration techniques were used to clean the once blackened and damaged stonework, revealing a building of astonishing delicacy and beauty.

Funding St Paul's

St Paul's receives no grants from central Government or from the Church. It costs about £13 million a year to fund the life of the cathedral; entry charges make a significant contribution towards the running costs, and the rest is raised through the diligent and persistent work of the St Paul's Foundation.

If you would like to know more about the cathedral's work, please visit us or view our website. We hope that from your visit to us you will take away something of the majesty of this building and our mission.

KEYS

The numbers listed relate to the multimedia guide available to cathedral visitors

THE CATHEDRAL FLOOR

1. The Baptismal Font
2. The Nave
3. The Dome Altar
4. The Dome
5. The Quire
6. Music track
7. The Quire and its Mosaics
8. The High Altar
9. Continuing your tour
10. Thornhill Paintings
11. Cleaning the Cathedral
12. The Cathedral and the Blitz, the North Transept
13. William Holman Hunt, *The Light of the World*
14. Henry Moore, *Mother and Child*
15. The Jesus Chapel dedicated to the American dead
16. Effigy of John Donne
17. John Howard monument
18. Fly-through of the Dome and Galleries
19. Accessing the Upper Galleries
20. Continuing your tour

THE CRYPT

1. Wellington's tomb
2. Falkland's memorial
3. The Chapel of St Faith's dedicated to the OBE
4. William Blake's memorial
5. John Everett Millais, JMW Turner and artists at St Paul's
6. Christopher Wren's tomb
7. Fly-through of the Great Model
8. The Previous Cathedrals
9. Arthur Sullivan and musicians at St Paul's
10. Alexander Fleming, Henry Wellcome and scientists at St Paul's
11. Nelson's tomb
12. Oculus
13. Winston Churchill memorial gates

KEY TO SYMBOLS

- **i** Information
- **♿** Accessible lift
- **♀♂** Toilets
- **S** Shop
- **⚲** Baby changing
- **◉** Oculus: An eye into St Paul's
- **☕** Café
- **🍽** Restaurant
- **𝌆** Stairs
- **◢** Ramp Access

THE GALLERIES

GOLDEN GALLERY
85 metres from Cathedral Floor
528 steps up

STONE GALLERY
53 metres from Cathedral Floor
376 steps up

WHISPERING GALLERY
30 metres from Cathedral Floor
257 steps up

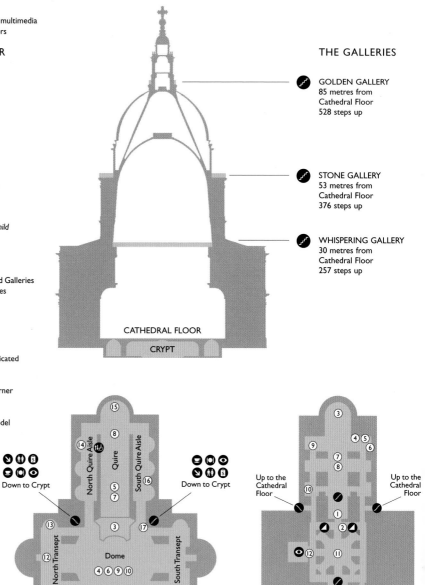

CATHEDRAL FLOOR

CRYPT

THE CATHEDRAL FLOOR

THE CRYPT

48